JOANNA - A fairly successful writer, she is bright and confident. Married to SEAN.

SEAN - JOANNA's husband, he is complacent but funny and caring.

BEN - A very successful writer, JOANNA's ex boyfriend, very dark sense of humour and sizable ego. Ben is deceased.

SCENE 1

Lights up on a kitchen. There is a table SL where they
sit to eat. SEAN is on stage, stood up with a bowl and
a spoon in his hand. JOANNA enters holding a large
clump of letters.

                SEAN
How strange, I was just about to sit
down with a bowl of beans, and you
appear! Although, unlike you, they are
cold, so I return them to the stove.

               JOANNA
That's a nice thing to say that I don't
understand.

Sifting through letters, she kisses him on the cheek.

           JOANNA (CONT'D)
What have you done today?

               SEAN
I put ice cream on my forehead.

               JOANNA
What?

               SEAN
I went to the shop earlier to get some
ice cream, had to walk back carrying a
few bags, and then when I got here, it
wouldn't fit in the freezer. So I had
to eat the whole tub myself before it
melted, and I was so hot that I took a
scoop and put it on my forehead.

               JOANNA
And just kind of...

               SEAN
Balanced it there.

                        JOANNA
          Did it work?

                        SEAN
          It really did.

She kisses his forehead.

                        JOANNA
          Shit.

                        SEAN
          What?

                        JOANNA
          I thought you were going to taste like
          ice cream.

                        SEAN
          Well I did wash afterwards.

                        JOANNA
          Yeah, I don't know why I assumed you
          wouldn't have.

                        SEAN
          Because you think I'm disgusting?

                        JOANNA
          You put cheese on your hot cross buns.

                        SEAN
          It's fucking good, all right?

                        JOANNA
          I will never believe you.

                        SEAN
          How can you know it's bad if you've
          never tried it?

JOANNA
I've never tried eating my own feet
either, but I can imagine it would be
unpleasant.

SEAN
Is that something you worry about?

JOANNA
What?

SEAN
Do you stay up at night, worrying that
your feet don't taste nice?

JOANNA
You're a ridiculous man.

SEAN
No, I mean, this is good, because it
means we've cut through the first six
months and got to the good stuff.

JOANNA
You want to analyse me now?

SEAN
Well that's not all I want to do to
you, but yes.

She looks up at him smiling.

SEAN (CONT'D)
See, I just took it to the next level.

JOANNA
So what are you doing tonight?

SEAN
Propositioning you.

JOANNA
After that.

                         SEAN
          Nothing really.
                    (Picking out two bags of
                     crisps from a cupboard)
          What about you?
                    (Throwing her the bag of
                     crisps)
          You going to do any writing?

                         JOANNA
          Shut up.

                         SEAN
          I'm just saying.

                         JOANNA
          Shut up.

                         SEAN
          I'm just saying, you have a lot to do
          and not a lot of time to do it in.

                         JOANNA
          And I'm just saying that I hate you.

                         SEAN
               (Long pause)
          Too mean!

                         JOANNA
          Eat your crisps.

SEAN opens his packet and starts to eat them.

                         SEAN
               (With a mouth full of crisps)
          Hey, I have my-

                         JOANNA
               (Interrupting)
          Don't talk with your mouth full.

He swallows.

                    SEAN
I have my interview tomorrow.

                    JOANNA
For what?

                    SEAN
Argos.

                    JOANNA
Argos? You're going to work in Argos.

                    SEAN
Hey we can't all be posh heads like you
with your fancy "career".

                    JOANNA
Posh heads?

                    SEAN
That's right.

                    JOANNA
You're lucky you have redeeming
qualities.

                    SEAN
List them.

                    JOANNA
I'll list them if you get the job.

                    SEAN
So suddenly a job at Argos isn't
beneath me!

                    JOANNA
At least you get to go into the magical
cave.

                    SEAN
Yeah, I think you're getting confused
between Argos and the Argonauts.

JOANNA opens her crisps.

                SEAN (CONT'D)
Actually that would be amazing.

                JOANNA
No I mean the cave where they keep all
the goods, in the back.

                SEAN
See, I'm getting a job, you should get
on with your work too.

                JOANNA
Shut up.

SEAN tries to take the crisps from her packet.

                JOANNA (CONT'D)
Piss off, these are
mine.

                SEAN
Knock knock.

                JOANNA
Wow.

                SEAN
What?

                JOANNA
Knock knock?

                SEAN
Yeah?

                JOANNA
We're doing knock knock jokes now?

                SEAN
You're such a snob.

                    JOANNA
This isn't a pitch is it?

                    SEAN
No.

                    JOANNA
Because I'm just saying, if this is a
pitch then you should quit while you're
very far behind.

                    SEAN
This isn't a pitch! Now let me tell my
joke.

                    JOANNA
Fine.

                    SEAN
Knock Knock.

                    JOANNA
Who's there?

                    SEAN
Jesus.

                    JOANNA
Jesus who?

                    SEAN
What do you mean Jesus who? I'm Jesus!
Your lord and saviour! You know, water
into wine, ringing any bells?

                    JOANNA
Have you been using modelling glue in
an enclosed space?

                    SEAN
I thought it was funny.

                    JOANNA
It's not.

                    SEAN
          It is, it's like, funny because it's so
          crap.

                    JOANNA
          I get it, you can tell me why it's
          supposed to be funny all the live long
          day, but you can't make me care.

                    SEAN
          You don't think bad jokes are funny?

                    JOANNA
          Things that start with the word bad
          usually have that effect on me.

                    SEAN
          See, I love shit like that.

                    JOANNA
          Bad jokes?

                    SEAN
          Yeah.

                    JOANNA
          You know you're an idiot right?

                    SEAN
          Yes, yes I do.

JOANNA laughs.

                    SEAN (CONT'D)
          Go on, what's the worst joke you've
          ever heard?

                    JOANNA
          Honestly?

                    SEAN
          Yeah.

                    JOANNA
All right.
        (Pause)
Knock knock.

                    SEAN
Who's there?

                    JOANNA
Jesus.

                    SEAN
Shut up.

                    JOANNA
    (Smiling)
You don't know what I was going to say.

                    SEAN
It's funny.

                    JOANNA
Did I laugh?

                    SEAN
No.

                    JOANNA
Well, so far it's not looking good for
you.

                    SEAN
If you're getting shot at, chances are
you're doing something right.

                    JOANNA
You're not getting shot at, you're
being an idiot.

                    SEAN
It's a fine line.

                    JOANNA
Not as fine as you think.

JOANNA opens one of the letters and begins to read it.

                    SEAN
          I think you didn't laugh on purpose
          because I tried to take your crisps.

                    JOANNA
          Shut up a minute.

                    SEAN
          You can have some of mine, I am nothing
          if not fair.

                    JOANNA
          Shut up.

                    SEAN
               (Pause)
          What is it?

                    JOANNA
          Shit.

                    SEAN
          What?

                    JOANNA
          A guy I used to know, he's died.

                    SEAN
          Shit Jo, who was he?

                    JOANNA
          An old boyfriend of mine. His name was
          Ben.

                    SEAN
          Were you close?

                    JOANNA
          At one point, yeah... but I haven't
          spoken to him in like eleven years.

                    SEAN
    Why are you getting a letter about it?

                    JOANNA
    It's from his lawyer.

                    SEAN
    His lawyer?

                    JOANNA
    Yeah, it says he filled out a preneed
    while he was alive.

                    SEAN
    What's that?

                    JOANNA
    It's where you arrange your own funeral
    before you die.

                    SEAN
    What does that have to do with you?

                    JOANNA
    It says here he requested to be buried
    with me.

SEAN laughs.

                    JOANNA (CONT'D)
    Shut up, this is horrible.

                    SEAN
    Is he threatening you?

                    JOANNA
    No. His lawyers just want me to sign a
    contract saying I'll be buried next to
    him.

                    SEAN
    Why would you do that?

                    JOANNA
          Because otherwise I don't get the money
          he left me.

                     SEAN
          Oh snap! How much?

                    JOANNA
          Doesn't say. Why would Ben want to be
          buried with me anyway?

                     SEAN
          Maybe he filled it out when you were
          still together.

                    JOANNA
          Yeah, I guess so. Still, it's a pretty
          weird step to take.

                     SEAN
          Did he know he was dying when he was
          with you?

                    JOANNA
          No. At least, I don't think so. I
          didn't know anyway, so if he did he
          didn't tell me.

                     SEAN
          We've got ourselves a mystery then! And
          some free money!

                    JOANNA
          Sean, show some respect, I used to love
          this guy.

                     SEAN
          We get free money! I love this guy!

                    JOANNA
          Can you just go?

                     SEAN
          Oh come on Jo, I was just pissing
          about.

JOANNA
Yeah, I know... I just think I want
to... you know... sit for a while.

SEAN
You sure?

JOANNA
Yeah. You don't mind do you?

SEAN
Course not. I'll just be upstairs if
you need me. Mind if I check on you
every so often?

JOANNA
(Laughing)
No.

SEAN
See you in an hour.

JOANNA
On the dot.

She smiles and he kisses her on the forehead.

SEAN exits.

BEN walks onto the stage. JOANNA sits reading her
letter and begins to play along with her memories of
conversations with BEN, at first just going along with
it, but then actively recreating the moments.

                    BEN
So I was talking to this girl I know
the other night, and she told me that
on Thursday night she'd been out with a
bunch of people, and she got a taxi
home on her own. And, she invited the
driver in with her and fucked him.
Which is a strange enough story, but
what's fantastic is that she seemed
really proud of the fact that she
managed to get the fare down by ten
pounds, but don't you think it's
hilarious, that he still charged her at
all?
        (Pause)
Just some girl I know.
        (Pause)
Exactly! Like, that was nice, but I
still need five quid. Fucking gold!

                    JOANNA
I can't believe you hang out with
people like that.

                    BEN
Well they're not my friends really,
they're just people I know.

                    JOANNA
I don't like that you have friends like
that.

                    BEN
Come on, you know some fucked up people
too, what about Brian?

                    JOANNA
Yeah, he was pretty weird. Did I tell
you about the time he had sex down a
back alley, with a woman who was
engaged, and had 2 kids, whilst people
watched them?

                    BEN
People watched?

                    JOANNA
          Yeah, her friends apparently.

                    BEN
          ...did they just.... see to themselves?

                    JOANNA
               (Laughing)
          I guess so.

                    BEN
          What would you give for it to have been
          her fiancé?

JOANNA laughs again.

                    BEN (CONT'D)
          OR HER KIDS!
               (Mimes masturbation)
          "God damnit, my mum is hot!"

JOANNA is now in hysterics.

                    JOANNA
          You can't fucking say
          that!

BEN laughs to himself.

                    BEN
          I should write that one
          down.

                    JOANNA
          I really don't think you should.

                    BEN
          Why not? You laughed.

                    JOANNA
          Yeah but I don't think most people
          would, they'd probably just be
          disturbed.

                          BEN
          I don't think you're giving people
          enough credit, they're plenty disturbed
          already.

JOANNA walks over, hugs and kisses him.

                          JOANNA
          I love you so much you know?

BEN smiles at her. There is a long pause.

                          JOANNA (CONT'D)
          So what's all this
          about?

                          BEN
          What's what about?

                          JOANNA
          You want to be buried with me?

                          BEN
          Yeah, this isn't how it went.

                          JOANNA
          Well yeah, I know that.

                          BEN
          This is unusual.

                          JOANNA
          Come on Ben, what's it about?

                          BEN
          I just... want to be buried with you.

                          JOANNA
          Why?

                    BEN
          Who cares why? It was my dying wish!

                    JOANNA
          It's a pretty gay one.

BEN laughs a little.

                    BEN
          I just wanted to be with you.

                    JOANNA
          We've been broken up for eleven years.

                    BEN
          Yeah, and how shit is that?

                    JOANNA
          Ben.

                    BEN
          This is me and you Jo, this is what I
          wanted. I wanted to be with you.

                    JOANNA
          Ben, you never even tried to get in
          touch with me.

                    BEN
          Well, you were with Jesus boy.

                    JOANNA
          Yeah, what the fuck was that?

                    BEN
             (Laughing)
          You tell me! You're with him.

                    JOANNA
He's a great guy, he
really is.

                    BEN
I have no doubt.

                    JOANNA
Hang on. How did you know I was with
him?

                    BEN
You told me about him when we met up
that day. You told me about this new
guy you'd been seeing and how you
thought it might "go the distance". It
was very insensitive.

                    JOANNA
Yeah, but you didn't know I was <u>still</u>
with him. You'd wait for death before
telling me you wanted to be with me?

                    BEN
Yeah, that's a good point.

                    JOANNA
        (Frustrated)
Ben!

                    BEN
I don't know, maybe I was too proud,
maybe I was going to but saw you
together. Maybe I followed you around
for a while to see if you were happy,
and concluded that you were.
        (Making his voice deeper)
Maybe I was waiting for you to get
bored of knock knock jokes and ice
cream, and come looking for a semi-
literate fuck-machine.

                    JOANNA
You're a fair way from being semi-
literate.

                    BEN
Yeah I know, I just always wanted to be
an alpha male.

                    JOANNA
            (Grinning)
You're going to be no help at all, are
you.

                    BEN
I don't think you brought me here to be
helpful.

JOANNA hugs him and closes her eyes.

                    JOANNA
I think you're right.

Lights go down.

                                    END SCENE

SCENE 2

JOANNA, SEAN and BEN are on stage, BEN is following
SEAN around.

> JOANNA
> I'm supposed to go see his lawyer
> tomorrow to find out what's going on.

> SEAN
> All the fun of the fair.

> JOANNA
> But with twice the vomit.

> SEAN
> Oh yes.

> JOANNA
> I hate going to see lawyers, I always
> feel like I'm being tricked into
> something. They always have a thinly
> veiled smirk. I swear, one day one of
> them is going to turn up and show me
> I've signed a contract that says "all
> milk is shit", and I can't drink it any
> more.

> SEAN
> (Laughing)
> Have you been tricked before?

> JOANNA
> Would I know if I had?

> SEAN
> No, but I'd know.

> JOANNA
> How?

                    SEAN
          I know everything.

                    JOANNA
          Shut up.

                    SEAN
          I once got tricked by a pigeon.

                    JOANNA
          A pigeon?

                    SEAN
          Yeah.

                    JOANNA
          Should I be sitting for this story?

BEN begins to walk around imitating a pigeon.

                    SEAN
          I was waiting to meet this girl.

                    JOANNA
          Oh really?

                    SEAN
          This was ages ago, before you.

                    JOANNA
          Nope. You were never with anybody
          before me.

                    SEAN
          This is in Joannaland?

                    JOANNA
          Yes.

                    SEAN
Okay, I was meeting this guy.

                    JOANNA
No no. That's worse. You were meeting a
tortoise.
      (Pronounced tor-toyss)

                    SEAN
A tortoise?
      (Pronounced tor-tuss)

                    JOANNA
It's tortoise.
      (Pronounced tor-toyss)

                    SEAN
It's clearly tortoise.
      (Pronounced tor-tuss)

                    JOANNA
It's O-I-S-E; voice isn't pronounced
vuss. It's clearly tortoise.

                    SEAN
You're wrong.

                    JOANNA
I'm never wrong.

                    SEAN
      (Pause)
So anyway, I was meeting this
nymphomaniac supermodel porn star, who
bought the moon and gave it to me as a
gift for being so unfalteringly
desirable, and had a weekly column in
the newspaper called "Musings" for
marathon sex and baking, when I saw
this pigeon.

                    JOANNA
That was a truly spectacular sentence.

                    SEAN
            (Acting out the story, miming
              the pigeon and the pillar)
        And this pigeon had a body that was too
        big for his head, it looked really
        funny. So I was sat on a bench laughing
        at it.

                    JOANNA
        Naturally.

                    SEAN
        When it walked behind a big pillar. I
        thought to myself, no problem, I can
        see both sides of this pillar, either
        way he walks or flies out I'll see him
        and I can laugh at him. About fifteen
        minutes pass, and I start wondering
        where he's gone.

                    JOANNA
        The supermodel was late?

                    SEAN
        Yeah.

                    JOANNA
        She wasn't a punctual porn star?

                    SEAN
        Her name was...
            (Stopping to look at her,
             smiling)
        Her name was
        Principessa.

                    JOANNA
        Principessa?

                    SEAN
        It means "of uncommon beauty".

        JOANNA laughs.

                    SEAN (CONT'D)
So I got up to investigate. Looked
behind the pillar, and the pigeon had
gone!

                    JOANNA
Principessa NOO!

                    SEAN
So I look around, and over to my left I
see the pigeon walking along, and this
is the good bit... Next to a guy
holding a suitcase!

JOANNA laughs loudly.

                    SEAN (CONT'D)
She was hiding behind the suitcase, to
stop me from being able to see her as
she snuck out from behind the pillar!

                    JOANNA
Principessa is a crafty bitch.

                    SEAN
That she is.

                    JOANNA
See what I did there?

                    SEAN
What?

                    JOANNA
I turned Principessa into the pigeon.

                    SEAN
So you did.

                    JOANNA
I'm the puppet master.

                    SEAN
They could both be called Principessa.

                    JOANNA
          (Sarcastically)
Yes. There might be two people called
Principessa.

                    SEAN
There might!

                    JOANNA
Are you trying to tell me that your
dream girl is a porn star pigeon whose
body is too fat for her head?

                    SEAN
Absolutely.

                    JOANNA
And yet you settled for me.

                    SEAN
Don't beat yourself up, you remind me
of a pigeon sometimes.

                    JOANNA
          (Laughing)
What?

                    SEAN
When you get surprised, you move your
head in really quick, sharp movements.
And when you see crumbs too.

                    JOANNA
I do not!

                    SEAN
You do!

He imitates the head movement of a pigeon.

                    SEAN (CONT'D)
Plus, the reason pigeons were
originally introduced to this country
was for food.

                    JOANNA
What does that have to do with
anything?

                    SEAN
Sometimes I want to cook you.

                    JOANNA
You want to what?

                    SEAN
Cook you.

                    JOANNA
You should be careful when you say
cook. I might have thought you said
something else.

                    SEAN
Oh really?

                    JOANNA
All this talk of pigeons getting you
hot?

                    SEAN
        (Pause)
What the hell are we talking about?

                    JOANNA
I was kind of hoping you'd know. Why
would you want to own the moon anyway?

                    SEAN
What?

                    JOANNA
You said your dream girl bought you the
moon.

                    SEAN
Yeah but I mean, what? You wouldn't
want to own the moon?

                    JOANNA
What possible reason could you have for
wanting to own the moon?

                    SEAN
I need somewhere to keep my sex pigeons
where you won't find them.

                    JOANNA
What makes you think I'm not into that?

                    SEAN
Eventually we're going to have to get
off this train of thought.

                    JOANNA
You'd rather talk about lawyers?

                    SEAN
I'd rather take your pigeony self
upstairs and pluck you.

                    BEN
This is graphic!

                    JOANNA
        (Pause)
Not while this Ben thing is going on. I
don't know why, it just seems weird.

                    SEAN
All right then.
        (As though calling to her)
Principessa!

                    JOANNA
You understand right?

                    SEAN
          Not really. But that's okay. You're a
          bit out of sorts, and I'm not gonna
          make that any harder for you. However,
          this shouldn't be taken as an
          indication that I don't fancy the shit
          out of you.

She laughs and kisses him.

                    JOANNA
          I'm gonna go do some work.

                    SEAN
          What are you going to write about?

                    JOANNA
          I dunno, maybe pigeons. Maybe all milk
          being shit.

                    SEAN
          Testify.

                    JOANNA
          I'm all about the truth.

                    SEAN
          Okay. I'll leave you to it.

JOANNA cannot think of anything to say in response to
this. SEAN smiles and exits, leaving BEN and JOANNA.

                    BEN
               (Long pause)
          I just ruin everything don't I.

                    JOANNA
          Shut up.

                                        LIGHTS FADE

                                        END SCENE

SCENE 3

SEAN is on stage, JOANNA enters.

                    SEAN
     How did it go?

                    JOANNA
     Not so good.

                    SEAN
     Did you sign it?

                    JOANNA
     No.

                    SEAN
     How come?

                    JOANNA
     Because. If I do then that's a binding
     contract, and I don't know if I want to
     be buried with him.

                    SEAN
     Not enough money to make it worth it?

                    JOANNA
     Yeah actually. It was eighty thousand
     pounds.

                    SEAN
     Shit yeah! Get me a wig, I'll fucking
     sign it!

                    JOANNA
     You wouldn't mind me being buried with
     an ex boyfriend?

                    SEAN
Of course I would, a little, but I
mean, it's more important to me that
you live well. So he gets to be with
you when you're dead. I get to
be with you while you're alive, that
seems like a fair trade off to me.

                    JOANNA
          (Smiling)
He got to be with me while he was alive
too.

                    SEAN
Well yeah, but he's more talented than
I am.

                    JOANNA
How do you know?

                    SEAN
          (Picking up a book from the
            table)
Picked up a copy of his book.

                    JOANNA
What? Why?

                    SEAN
It's hilarious!

                    JOANNA
Why did you buy it?

                    SEAN
Wanted to check out the competition.

                    JOANNA
He's not competition, he's dead.

                    SEAN
I'm not saying I don't like my chances.

                    JOANNA
You want to hear the weird thing?

                    SEAN
        (Laughing)
This isn't weird so far?

                    JOANNA
He only got the preneed done three
years ago.

                    SEAN
Not while you were still together?

                    JOANNA
Nope.

                    SEAN
Which was eleven years ago right?

                    JOANNA
Yeah.

                    SEAN
So after you hadn't seen each other for
seven years, he suddenly signs this
agreement?

                    JOANNA
Seven plus three is ten you idiot.

                    SEAN
        (Pauses)
Oh my god.... what's happened to me?
What the shit happened there?

                    JOANNA
And no...

                    SEAN
Seven plus three is ten.

                    JOANNA
Sean.

                    SEAN
Seven plus three has always been ten.

                    JOANNA
I saw him more recently than that.

                    SEAN
When?

                    JOANNA
...About three years ago.

                    SEAN
    (Pause)
While we were together?

                    JOANNA
Yes.

                    SEAN
And that's when he wrote up this
agreement?

                    JOANNA
Yes.

                    SEAN
What are you saying Jo?

                    JOANNA
Nothing.

                    SEAN
Did anything happen between you?

                    JOANNA
No, nothing at all.

                    SEAN
Really?

                    JOANNA
I swear.

                    SEAN
I want to know.

                    JOANNA
I said nothing happened. You don't
believe me?

                    SEAN
Hey, I don't mean to be a dick here,
but you going to visit him and then him
deciding he still loves you enough to
want to be buried with you... You must
have done something to make him think
you'd get back together. I don't think
I'm out of line here for being a little
suspicious. Especially when you didn't
tell me about it. Why is that? And why,
if it was serious enough to warrant him
wanting to lie beside you forever, has
he never been mentioned until now?

                    JOANNA
We just had dinner.

                    SEAN
Three years ago is when you proposed to
me. What was that? Out of guilt for
fucking someone else?

                    JOANNA
I didn't fuck him!

                    SEAN
He just happened to take it as a sign
you'd be buried with him? It's one of
those signals you think won't be
important, but if you get it wrong it
can really
        (Shouting)
fuck you over.

                    JOANNA
Listen to me Ben, nothing happened!

                    SEAN
                (Long pause)
            I'm Sean.

                    JOANNA
            Yeah, I should have been able to tell;
            Ben would have trusted me.

                    SEAN
                (Very long
                 pause)
            I'm going to walk away
            now.

                    JOANNA
            Sean, I'm sorry.

He starts to walk out, BEN walks in and sits down at
the table.

                    JOANNA (CONT'D)
            Sean, talk to me, shout at me- do
            something...

                    SEAN
            What? What do you want? Closure? You
            want to be able to feel like the fight
            is over? Fuck you.

He walks out, she turns around and sits opposite BEN.

                    BEN
            You know what I'm getting sick of?
                (Pause)
            Horror films where the monster is just
            a kid with weird eyes.

                    JOANNA
            Go away.

                    BEN
          I'm telling you now, I don't care how
          many demons it's possessed by, I could
          kick an eight year old's ass. Not only
          that, but as far as I'm concerned, if a
          kid shows up in a dimly lit room,
          they're just asking for it.

JOANNA is still upset, but plays along.

                    JOANNA
          I don't think that would make as good a
          film, just you beating up kids in a
          dark room.

                    BEN
          I could make it more interesting I
          suppose. Me killing kids in a dark
          room... WITH A FLAMETHROWER.

JOANNA snickers.

                    BEN (CONT'D)
          Huh? Wait... he's not burning! Damnit!
          I KNEW black people didn't have souls!

JOANNA laughs though she is obviously still upset.

                    BEN (CONT'D)
          Come on! If you're going to play do it
          properly, you weren't crying. Sort
          yourself out.

                    JOANNA
          Ben, you are fucked! It's not okay to
          joke about that.

                    BEN
          You're laughing!

                    JOANNA
          That's not the point.

                    BEN
The point is, not talking about racism
isn't doing anybody any good. If we
really want to get rid of it, we need
to make it hilarious.

                    JOANNA
You don't know what you're talking
about.

                    BEN
We need to make it so that the very
idea of being racist is so idiotic,
that nobody can take it seriously.

                    JOANNA
Whether you're right or-

                    BEN
I am.

                    JOANNA
Whether you're right or not... That is
just not your call to make.

                    BEN
Yeah, I hate not being a dictator.

                    JOANNA
I bet you do.

                    BEN
Stalin wouldn't have this problem.

                    JOANNA
He had a few problems of his own.

                    BEN
          Speaking of Stalin, I was in a Chinese
          takeaway the other day, and on the wall
          they had this calendar of the Chinese
          zodiac. And I read some of it, and the
          one for the year of the rabbit said "A
          natural leader, but can be prone to
          moodiness" and under it, there was a
          list of famous people born of this
          sign. And guess who was on it.

                    JOANNA
          Stalin.

                    BEN
          Not only him, Stalin and Castro.
          Leadership, maybe, but prone to
          moodiness? That's ridiculous!

She laughs and there is a pause in the conversation.

                    JOANNA
          Oh yeah, I'm writing a book.

                    BEN
          Yeah?

                    JOANNA
          Yeah well, I've always wanted to be
          thinly veiled, and it's got to the
          point where this is the only way I can
          see it happening.

                    BEN
          You never know, I could write something
          with you in it.

                    JOANNA
          I don't think I could handle being in
          one of yours; you'd make my eyelids out
          of dominoes.

                    BEN
          That would be so hot.

                    JOANNA
Ben.

                    BEN
No don't talk don't ruin
it.

She laughs.

                    JOANNA
Are you here to cheer me up?

                    BEN
What do you mean?

                    JOANNA
After my fight with Sean.

                    BEN
        (Theatrically)
Who's Sean?

                    JOANNA
You know who Sean is.

                    BEN
You expect me to be able to tell
between when I'm a memory and when I'm
saying something new?

                    JOANNA
        (Pause)
Yes actually, I do.

                    BEN
Yeah you're right, I can.

                    JOANNA
Then why are you giving me a hard time?

                    BEN
I dunno; tradition mostly.

                    JOANNA
Are you here to cheer me up?

                    BEN
Well, either that or make you even more
mad at him by being wonderful.

                    JOANNA
    (Pause)
It is kind of working that way.

                    BEN
Jo, you're not an idiot, you know
you've edited out all the bad bits of
our relationship, and that's why I seem
great.

                    JOANNA
I haven't edited them out, I'm just
choosing not to focus on them right
now.

                    BEN
Probably not the healthiest attitude to
take.

                    JOANNA
You can't talk to me about health,
you're dead.

                    BEN
I meant emotional health.

                    JOANNA
    (Pause)
You killed yourself.

                    BEN
No, I might have killed myself, you
don't know for sure.

                    JOANNA
They said...

BEN
They said it was inconclusive! Does it
seem like something I'd do?

JOANNA
No.

BEN
You should give him a break.

JOANNA
Who, Sean?

BEN
Yeah. Think about it, it does look
pretty suspicious. Just let him know
calmly, that nothing happened.

JOANNA
(She smiles)
Why didn't we work?

BEN
(Jokingly)
Because I hated you.

JOANNA laughs.

BEN (CONT'D)
I mean it, I really hated you.

JOANNA
Shut up.

BEN
Go talk to him.

JOANNA
Alright, I will.

LIGHTS GO DOWN

END SCENE

SCENE 4

Lights go up on SEAN and JOANNA mid conversation.

                    SEAN
        All right, all right. I believe you, I
        do. It's just... hard to shake that
        kind of thing. I know I should… it's
        just hard to shake that kind of thing.

                    JOANNA
        I promise you, nothing happened.

                    SEAN
        All right then.

                    JOANNA
        Actually, I spent most of the day
        talking about you.

                    SEAN
            (Grinning a little)
        Oh really?

                    JOANNA
        Yes.

                    SEAN
        Bet he liked that.

                    JOANNA
        Well I know I did.

                    SEAN
        So what did you say?

                    JOANNA
        I said, that I was really happy I'd
        found you, and that really, I couldn't
        ask for anyone better.

                    SEAN
               (Smiling)
          It might be nice if you told me that
          every so often.

                    JOANNA
          I tell you sometimes.

                    SEAN
          Yeah but you could write me some poems
          and stuff, really do it up.

                    JOANNA
          Oh really?

                    SEAN
          Yeah!

                    JOANNA
          Well where are my poems then?

                    SEAN
          You know I can't write mushy love
          poems.

                    JOANNA
          Then write creamy hate psalms.

                    SEAN
               (Laughing)
          It's not that. I lost a bet a long time
          ago, and now for the rest of my life,
          every time I write a poem, the last
          line has to be "Here I am, rock you
          like a hurricane".

     JOANNA laughs.

                    SEAN (CONT'D)
          And I think you'll find that the most
          moving of all sentiment would be
          blunted by such a statement.

                    JOANNA
Well they're not going to know you
wrote it.

                    SEAN
Doesn't matter! I'm a man of my word.
If I'd have won, I'd have expected him
to do it forever.

                    JOANNA
Fine, I'll let you off.

                    SEAN
Did Ben ever write you poems?

                    JOANNA
Oh please. Ben wrote the original song
"Rock you like a hurricane".

                    SEAN
You trying to make me jealous?

                    JOANNA
Yeah, you should be fighting for me.

                    SEAN
He's dead. I'm calling that a win.

There is an awkward moment, and JOANNA looks down at
the floor.

                    SEAN (CONT'D)
Shit Jo, I'm sorry.

                    JOANNA
It's all right.

                    SEAN
No I mean it. I know this must be
harder for you than you're letting on.

                    JOANNA
Really, it's fine.

                    SEAN
        (Pause)
Do you know how he died?

                    JOANNA
        (Long pause)
He killed himself.

                    SEAN
Oh, fuck.

                    JOANNA
Well. It was inconclusive really. But
the coroner said he was pretty sure.

                    SEAN
Does it seem like something he'd do?

                    JOANNA
        (Smiling a little)
It really doesn't. He was far too...
stubborn for that.

                    SEAN
So you think he didn't do it?

                    JOANNA
I really don't know. I just know that I
can't imagine it.

                    SEAN
        (Long pause)
What else did you say about me?

                    JOANNA
Sean.

                    SEAN
No, bear with me.

                    JOANNA
              (A little annoyed)
I told him, that I could see wanting to
be with you forever.

                    SEAN
...and then a few days later, he went
and got the contract done.

                    JOANNA
What are you getting at?

                    SEAN
He's trying to fuck us!

                    JOANNA
What?

                    SEAN
He is trying to fuck us!

                    JOANNA
What do you mean?

                    SEAN
I mean, since you found out about this
we've been living day by day! You've
been thinking about him again, we had a
big argument, he's trying to split us
up.

                    JOANNA
You're a fucking child.

                    SEAN
Think about it.

                    JOANNA
He would never do that.

              SEAN
Think about it. He asks you to come
meet him, wants to talk to you, you
tell him you have a new boyfriend, you
tell him how great it's all going, and
then he goes away, signs a contract
saying he wants to be buried with you
and then kills himself.

              JOANNA
He didn't <u>then</u> kill himself; there were
three years between that and us
meeting. And anyway, he didn't kill
himself.

              SEAN
Oh really, because the coroner was
pretty sure.

              JOANNA
I know him, he wouldn't do that. He was
too stubborn, he would never do that.

              SEAN
Unless he had an ulterior motive.

              JOANNA
Shut up, seriously just shut the fuck
up. You think he's trying to... I loved
him, and he loved me. You don't think
there might be some other reason he
might want to be buried with me?

              SEAN
    (Shocked, pauses then shouts)
No!

              JOANNA
Oh fuck you, you know why that is?

              SEAN
Why.

                    JOANNA
Because you can't love. The entire
romantic side of you can be buttered
onto a clichéd slideshow of mixed tapes
and trepanation. Me and Ben, we loved
each other by the throat. We couldn't
stand it, it was choking us.

                    SEAN
You're saying you loved him more than
me?

                    JOANNA
Yeah, well, now we both have a scar we
can talk about.

                    SEAN
        (Pacing)
If you loved him so much, why didn't it
work?

                    JOANNA
I don't know why, he won't tell me.

                    SEAN
He won't tell you? Jesus Jo, you are
fucked.

                    JOANNA
You're fucking right I am! Don't you
get it? Ben is gone, the guy I loved is
gone.
        (Pause)
Ben didn't care about much but he cared
about me, and I think the least I can
do for him is let people know just how
fucked up I am that he's dead!

JOANNA exits.

                            LIGHTS GO DOWN

                            END SCENE

SCENE 5

JOANNA is going about their business in the house,
obviously awkward. SEAN is sat at the table reading
BEN's book and making conversation. BEN is sat
opposite SEAN.

>   SEAN
>   Had my interview today.

>   JOANNA
>   How did it go?

>   SEAN
>   Not well.

>   JOANNA
>   Really?

>   SEAN
>   Yeah. I kept... I kept laughing at
>   them.

>   JOANNA
>   Why?

>   SEAN
>   I didn't mean to. It was just, he was
>   taking the notes for what I said, using
>   one of those tiny blue Argos pens.

BEN starts laughing.

>   JOANNA
>   Oh Sean.

>   BEN
>   It's funny!

>   SEAN

I know. And every time I answered a
question and he started writing with
it, I just laughed again.

SEAN is smiling JOANNA is not amused, BEN is laughing.

                    SEAN (CONT'D)
          Sorry Jo. I'll go out tomorrow and find
          another interview, we'll be fine.

                    JOANNA
          It's alright.

                    BEN
          I would have laughed.

                    JOANNA
          Do me a favour, don't read that shit in
          front of me.

                    BEN
          Excuse me, shit?

                    SEAN
          I see you're in it.

                    JOANNA
          Am I?

                    SEAN
          You didn't know?

                    JOANNA
          That's a newer one, I didn't read the
          newer ones.

                    SEAN
          Why not?

                    JOANNA
          Didn't feel right.

                    SEAN
          Fair enough.

                    JOANNA
          (Long pause)
     I'm in it?

                    SEAN
     Yeah. And I'm not positive, but I think
     I might be too.

                    JOANNA
     Why?

                    SEAN
     You, your name is Emma, meet a guy
     because of a wobbly piece of stone.
          (Long pause)
     How does he know about that?

                    JOANNA
     I told him when we met up.

                    SEAN
     Why did you tell him that?

                    JOANNA
     Why wouldn't I? It's a funny story, I
     was telling him about you.

                    SEAN
     Yeah but it's our story. It's mine and
     yours, I don't want him having it.

                    BEN
     What the hell is he talking about?

                    JOANNA
     I'm sorry.

                    SEAN
              (Pausing a moment then
                smiling)
          No, it's fine. I don't know why I just
          did that, I tell that story all the
          time. I don't know why I just did that.

SEAN goes back to reading and JOANNA walks towards a
cupboard and pulls out a bag of crisps, while BEN
pushes himself along the floor on his back.

                    JOANNA
          Weird that he'd put us in it.

                    SEAN
          You know what's weirder?

                    JOANNA
          What?

                    SEAN
          That my character, whose name is Paul,
          seems to be allergic to wonder.

SEAN smiles up at her, JOANNA laughs.

                    SEAN (CONT'D)
          Perhaps some misplaced aggression
          there.

                    BEN
          I'll misplace your head.

JOANNA throws the crisps to him and he begins to eat
them.

                    SEAN
          You think I could take him?

                    BEN
          What?

                    JOANNA
          What?

                    SEAN
Do you think I could take him, in a
fight?

                    JOANNA
Yeah.

                    BEN
WHAT!?

                    JOANNA
I think you could take him.

                    BEN
Yeah, to dinner maybe. Fuck you!

                    JOANNA
Do you think you could take him?

                    SEAN
I don't know. Never met him, haven't
figured him out yet.

                    JOANNA
What do you mean?

                    SEAN
Every time I meet someone I
instinctively figure out how to fight
them.

                    JOANNA
        (Laughing)
Really?

                    SEAN
Yeah.

                    JOANNA
How would you fight me?

                    SEAN
When you stand, you put all your weight
on your left leg so your right side is

vulnerable. Lean in to take momentum
off your hits, then bam!

                    JOANNA
          (Softly)
     You're a ridiculous man.

                    SEAN
          (Pause)
     Maybe, but I could beat you up.

                    JOANNA
     I'm not so sure you know, I'm spry.

                    SEAN
     Ha! I've already won before we even
     start.

                    JOANNA
     I don't think so boy. I have a fire in
     my soul, and I will take you down!

                    SEAN
     Ooh, I like a woman with ambition. It's
     like watching a dog try to wear
     clothes.

JOANNA laughs loudly.

                    JOANNA
     That was funny.

                    SEAN
          (Pauses a while then admits)
     Paul said it.

                    JOANNA
     Paul?

                    SEAN
     My character from Ben's book.

                    JOANNA
     I knew it!

                    SEAN
     Yeah. In a way, I have writers now.

                    JOANNA
Not anymore.

                    SEAN
That's true.

                    JOANNA
I knew it sounded more like Ben.

                    SEAN
Oh really?

                    JOANNA
Yeah.

                    SEAN
Because, for me to say something funny
would be surprising.

                    JOANNA
Ooh, shut up. All I meant was Ben has a
very distinct sense of humour.

                    BEN
Shit yeah I do.

                    SEAN
And I don't?

                    JOANNA
You know what I mean.

                    SEAN
          (Putting on squeaky voice)
You know what I mean bllblblblll.
          (Voice back to normal)
That's you, that's how dumb you sound.

JOANNA laughs slightly.

                    JOANNA
You know I think you're funny.

                    BEN
          I'm funnier.

                    SEAN
          Sorry, what was that? I wasn't really
          listening, I was trying to work out a
          vocal pitch to patronising tone ratio.
          Keep talking, I'm almost there.

                    BEN
          That was shit. I'm better.

                    JOANNA
          Are you going to be making jokes all
          day now?

                    SEAN
          Like that would be such a bad thing.

                    BEN
          I could teach him to be funny.

                    JOANNA
          Are you really insecure about this?

                    BEN
          Let me teach him.

                    SEAN
          No.

                    JOANNA
          I know you, I know when something's
          bothering you. Why do you care?

                    BEN
          Seriously, let me teach him. I can be
          the Robin Williams to his school kids
          who learn that killing yourself is the
          best way to live for the moment.

                    SEAN
          I don't, I'm fine.

                    BEN
Live for the moment Sean, live for the
moment.

                  JOANNA
You don't have to worry about not being
funny.

                    SEAN
I don't worry about that.

                    BEN
Carpe diem you wanker.

                  JOANNA
Is this something to do with your dad?

                    SEAN
No. It isn't.

                  JOANNA
Ok.

                    SEAN
     (Pause)
Okay, I can see you're trying to open
me up right now, and that's great, but
I'm pretty much done talking.

                  JOANNA
It's okay to talk about it.

                    SEAN
Talk about what?

                  JOANNA
Your dad.

SEAN

Oh for God's sake, I don't have daddy
issues, I have fucking... you issues!
Ok?

JOANNA

I don't believe you.

SEAN

I know you don't. I know you, and I
know you're going to go upstairs to
your books and start researching who I
am and what I want, but in the meantime
the sky is falling, and you and me
can't eat a bag of crisps without
coughing up the ball.

JOANNA

The ball?

SEAN

Yes.

JOANNA

The ball? Conversations with me are
like sport? You work up a sweat trying
to prove yourself?

SEAN

It's an expression and you know it.

JOANNA

Yes, I do know it, but it's also so
incredibly like you to use that
expression. It's a sport, it's a game.
Why is everything a competition with
you?

SEAN

Why is everything a fight with you? Why
can't you accept it when things are
fine? Why is everything a fight with
you?

                    BEN
        Because you're damaged.

                    JOANNA
                (Shouting)
        Because you're damaged!

    There is a pause, then SEAN quickly exits.

                    JOANNA (CONT'D)
                (She shakes her head)
        You're right, you're so right! He is
        damaged!

                    BEN
        I was talking to you!

                    JOANNA
                (Pause)
        What?

                    BEN
        I was talking to you. And you know what
        else? You heard me. Think about that.

    BEN exits and JOANNA calls to SEAN. SEAN enters but
    stays quiet.

                    JOANNA
        Sean. I'm sorry for saying that.
                (Pause)
        I didn't even mean it. I think maybe I
        just wanted to, to fight about
        something. I don't know why. Lately
        I've just wanted to be angry. Are we
        okay?

                    SEAN
Yeah. We're okay. We're okay. But
that's all we are. We're okay. I want
us to be better than okay, I want us to
be great.
          (Looking intently at her)
It's not all this shit. This is just
something that's going on. It's that
the time to go between us getting on
great to us unable to have a
conversation could have been clocked
with an egg timer. What do we do about
that?

                              LIGHTS GO DOWN

                                 END SCENE

SCENE 6

BEN and JOANNA are sat at a table in a cafe.

                    BEN
        You met because of a wobbly piece of
        stone?

                    JOANNA
        I told you you'd love this story.

                    BEN
        What happened?

                    JOANNA
        I was stood there outside the train
        station waiting for my friend, when I
        noticed I was standing on one of those
        wobbly slabs of paving that go down a
        bit when you step on them. So I decide,
        while I'm waiting, I'll put all my
        weight onto one half of the slab. That
        way I can see if people who step on it
        can lift me up. Like see if they're
        heavier than me, or put more force on
        or whatever. So I'm stood on it, and
        then this guy walks past, stands on the
        slab and then instead of carrying on
        walking, he slows down and turns to
        look at me. Says to me "Are you putting
        all your weight on that stone?" He
        tells me that he walks this way every
        day and making that stone wobble is
        part of his ritual, and I've ruined it.

                    BEN
        He said that to a
        stranger?

                    JOANNA
            (Laughing)
        Yeah.

                    BEN
I have to meet this guy.

                    JOANNA
You really do, he's such a great guy.
Anyway, we end up getting a toastie in
a café. And then we've been together
ever since.

                    BEN
As jealous as I am, that's still the
best chance encounter story I've ever
heard.

                    JOANNA
You'd love him.

                    BEN
I don't think I would.

                    JOANNA
He's lovely.

                    BEN
I'm sure he is, but I'm biased.

                    JOANNA
        (Laughing)
I guess so.

                    BEN
Also, lovely is a bit effeminate. I
wouldn't say it in front of him.

                    JOANNA
I could really see this going all the
way, you know? I really could.

                    BEN
        (Long pause)
Well, that's great Jo, but it kind of
fucks up what I invited you here to
say.

                    JOANNA
          Ben, I thought you were just kidding
          around.

                     BEN
          Come on, I don't kid around.

She looks up at him.

                  BEN (CONT'D)
          Alright, I kid around all the time.
          But...

                    JOANNA
          Ben.

                     BEN
          I love you, I still love you.

                    JOANNA
          Ben, you'll love anyone who makes you
          feel like you're a better person than
          you are.

                     BEN
               (Long pause)
          That's the worst thing you've ever said
          to me.

                    JOANNA
          Why am I here?

                     BEN
          I just told you.

                    JOANNA
          Fuck off, Ben. Why am I here? Why now?

                     BEN
          Because I had to tell you, I had to let
          you know.

                         JOANNA
          I don't want to be with you.

                           BEN
          Why not?

                         JOANNA
          Because I've done it before.

                           BEN
          We work.

                         JOANNA
          We don't work.

                           BEN
          We could work this time.

                         JOANNA
          Why would it be different this time?

                           BEN
          Because you've grown.

                         JOANNA
               (Pause)
          I've grown?

                           BEN
          Yes you have, and we could make it
          work.

                         JOANNA
          You think I was the reason it didn't
          work out?

                           BEN
          I don't want to get into that.

                         JOANNA
          Get into it!

                    BEN
I don't want to.

                  JOANNA
You think it was my fault?

                    BEN
Of course it was your fault! You never
gave us a chance... you never put
anything in, you never allowed yourself
to be in it for us.

                  JOANNA
What a load of bilge.

                    BEN
It's true.

                  JOANNA
You think I didn't put enough of myself
into it? You have no concept of what it
was like for me, or how hard it was for
me to leave, you think I didn't put
myself into it? I loved you so much, I
loved the salt on your chips, I loved
the skin on your porridge, how dare you
say to me that I never allowed myself
to be in it for you.

                    BEN
Then what went wrong?

                  JOANNA
You got cold, that's what went wrong.
You got cold right after my book came
out. When you got published I was
strutting, I was strutting! Look what
my boyfriend did, my boyfriend is an
author. When mine came out you showed
me nothing but the back of your hand.

                    BEN
So you showed me the door?

                    JOANNA
You opened the door and you pulled me
over to it, you just didn't want to be
the one to leave because you're the guy
who stays. I had to be the one who
left.

                    BEN
That is bullshit.

                    JOANNA
It's true.

                    BEN
That is bull shit, I got cold because
you got so engrossed in your own
success that you forgot who I was.

                    JOANNA
My success? You were always more
successful than me.

                    BEN
And you hated me for it.

                    JOANNA
I loved you for everything you had. You
got cold, you hated me.

                    BEN
Yes, okay? Yes I hated you.

                    JOANNA
Why?

                    BEN
          Because you were better than me.
               (Long pause)
          I hated you, because you were better
          than me, you were always going to be
          better than me. And I couldn't handle
          that.

                  JOANNA
          You hated me?

                    BEN
          I loved you. But we worked, when we
          first got together, because you looked
          up to me, and I needed that. The time
          we were together, I needed it, I needed
          to feel like I was going to make an
          impact on someone's life.

                  JOANNA
          You loved me because I was weak?

                    BEN
          I needed you because I needed to feel
          strong.

JOANNA stands up.

                  JOANNA
          Fuck you.

                    BEN
          I love you.

                  JOANNA
          I'm leaving. Don't ever contact me
          again.

JOANNA begins to leave.

                    BEN
          And that was it.

She stops and turns around.

                    JOANNA
          That was it.

                    BEN
          I never contacted you again.

                    JOANNA
          Until now.

                    BEN
          I'm not sure this counts.

JOANNA grins at him.

                    BEN (CONT'D)
          You told him you loved me more.

                    JOANNA
          It was just different.

                    BEN
          Why did you leave?

                    JOANNA
          Because you, are a fucked up guy. You
          are fucked up, and you would have
          dragged me down, and I knew that and it
          was still the hardest decision I have
          ever had to make. I wanted to be
          dragged down, I just couldn't let
          myself. Did you kill yourself?

                    BEN
          No.

                    JOANNA
          Sean doesn't believe you. He thinks all
          this is just a ploy to break us up.

                    BEN
          Maybe it is.

                    JOANNA
I don't believe it is.

                     BEN
Then why do you think I did it?

                    JOANNA
I think you never gave up thinking I'd
come back. I think you wanted us to be
together forever.

                     BEN
That's what I think too.

                    JOANNA
Why didn't you get in touch?

                     BEN
You didn't want me to.

                    JOANNA
Then what made you think I'd sign this?

                     BEN
That didn't matter. The important part
was getting you to see it.

                    JOANNA
Well I saw it.

                     BEN
     (Pause)
Are you going to sign it?

                    JOANNA
Yes.

                     BEN
What about Sean?

                    JOANNA
What about him?

                    BEN
He thinks this is all a plan to break
you up.

                    JOANNA
Then he's going to be glad it didn't
work.

                    BEN
You're going to stay with him, after
telling him you loved me more?

                    JOANNA
I didn't mean that. I love Sean. But
it's different. With me and you, there
was more stomach to it. I guess because
I was in awe of you. You were this
edgy, funny, successful guy, and I
thought your shit kept the world warm.
And we worked because you knew that's
how I felt. But when I knew myself
better, that wasn't the case anymore. I
still loved you, but you were human.
And you didn't want to be human, you
wanted to be the person I thought would
save the world. It's different with
Sean. Not just because we're older. He
isn't as funny or successful as you,
but our relationship works. We make
each other laugh, we help each other
out, and we know each other. And yes
it's different to what me and you had
but, that's all it is. Different, it's
not less. This isn't just what is best
for me, this is what makes me happy. I
see people, dreaming of fast love, that
will just envelope them. Then when they
don't find it, or it doesn't work out,
they settle for something else and
they're always a little bit... less for
it. But the dirty little secret is
that, the love they settled for is no
less romantic than what they had in
their heads all along, and you know

                        JOANNA (CONT'D)
          what? It's no less exciting either.
          What people have trouble realising is
          that the real world is exactly as
          fascinating as anything they could come
          up with. And me and Sean are exactly as
          in love as you and I were. It's just
          different.

                        BEN
          So you're going to work out?

                        JOANNA
          Yeah. We are.

                        BEN
               (Long pause)
          Fuck ye then.

     JOANNA laughs.

                        BEN (CONT'D)
          Go talk to him.

                        JOANNA
          Go rot in the ground.

                        BEN
               (Laughing)
          I will. And someday you'll be rotting
          with me.

                        JOANNA
          Goodbye, Ben.

     JOANNA walks off the stage and the lights fade.

                                        END SCENE

SCENE 7

Lights up on an empty stage. JOANNA and SEAN are stood
looking down at the same spot on the stage.

                    SEAN
          It was a nice service.

                    JOANNA
          I'm surprised you came. Glad, but
          surprised.

                    SEAN
          So you signed it then?

                    JOANNA
          I did.

                    SEAN
          Why?

                    JOANNA
          Because he was an important part of my
          life, however long ago it was. And
          because it was his dying wish.

                    SEAN
          Alright.

                    JOANNA
               (Long pause)
          Went to see my own lawyer yesterday.

                    SEAN
          What for?

                    JOANNA
          To make sure there wasn't already a
          book out there called "All milk is
          shit".

SEAN laughs quietly.

                    JOANNA (CONT'D)
          I picked up something for you as well.

JOANNA hands him a letter. After he has read it for a
while, she passes him a pen. He takes it from her and
looks down at it, then at her.

                    JOANNA (CONT'D)
                (Awkwardly)
          Of course, you can think about it for a
          while.

                         SEAN
          Thanks.

                    JOANNA
                (Quietly, almost in tears)
          It's okay.

                         SEAN
          Turn around.

                    JOANNA
          What?

                         SEAN
          Turn around.

                    JOANNA
          Why?

                         SEAN
          Just, turn around.

JOANNA turns around to face away from the audience.
SEAN grabs her waist and turns her 90 degrees so she
is facing away from him. He places the paper against
her back and signs it. JOANNA turns back to face the
audience and they look down at the ground again in the
same spot. They slowly begin to smile. There is an
extremely long pause.

                    SEAN (CONT'D)
        You're gonna look like a super stud
        with two guys buried next to you.

                    JOANNA
        You had to ruin the moment didn't you.

                    SEAN
        Yes, yes I did.
            (Pause)
        What are you going to spend the money
        on?

                    JOANNA
        Well some of it's gone already.

                    SEAN
        Already? What did you buy?

JOANNA pulls out another piece of paper. SEAN looks at
it and his eyes light up.

                    SEAN (CONT'D)
        AN ACRE OF THE MOON!

                    JOANNA
        An acre of the moon.

                    SEAN
            (Singing)
        I own the moon.

                    JOANNA
        A bit of the moon.

SEAN and JOANNA exit with SEAN repeating the word
moon, singing in a deep voice.

                    SEAN
        Moon moon moon moon moon moon moon.

                    JOANNA
          Please stop that.

                    SEAN
          I shall call it, PRINCIPESSA!

THEY BOTH EXIT THE STAGE TOGETHER AND THE LIGHTS FADE

                                        END SCENE

                                        END OF SCRIPT

Printed in Great Britain by
Amazon.co.uk, Ltd.,
Marston Gate.